Visiting Exile

Also by John Welch:

A Place Like Here (Katabasis, London 1968)
Six of Five (The Many Press, London 1975)
Wanting To Be Here (The X Press, London 1976)
The Fish God Problem (The Many Press, London 1977)
Braiding the Squadron (The Many Press, London 1977)
And Ada Ann, A Book of Narratives
                    (Great Works Press, Bishops Stortford 1978)
Performance (The Many Press, London 1979)
Grieving Signal (The Many Press, London 1980)
The Storms / Lip Service (The Many Press, London 1980)
Out Walking (Anvil, London 1984)
Erasures (The Many Press, London 1991)
Blood and Dreams (Reality Street Editions, London 1991)
Its Radiance (Poetical Histories, Cambridge 1993)
Glyph (Grille, London 1995)
Greeting Want (infernal methods, Cambridge 1997)
The Eastern Boroughs (Shearsman Books, Exeter 2004)
British Estate (AARK Arts, London & Delhi 2004)
On Orkney (infernal methods, Stromness 2005)
Collected Poems (Shearsman Books, Exeter, 2008)

Prose

Dreaming Arrival (Shearsman Books, Exeter, 2008)

As editor:

Stories from South Asia (Oxford University Press, 1984)

JOHN WELCH

Visiting Exile

Shearsman Books
Exeter

First published in the United Kingdom in 2009 by
Shearsman Books Ltd
58 Velwell Road
Exeter EX4 4LD

www.shearsman.com

ISBN   978-1-84861-076-7
First Edition

Acknowledgements

'British Estate' appeared as a pamphlet of that title from Aark Arts
and the sections 'On Murder Mile' and 'Home Ground'
as a pamphlet ,'Untold Wealth', from Oystercatcher Press.

Acknowledgement is also due to the editors of the following print
and online magazines where other sections have appeared in *Black Box
Manifold, Fire, Great Works, Intercapillary Space, nthposition, Tears in the Fence,
Shadowtrain* and *Signals.*

Translation from Ghalib reproduced by courtesy of
the Estate of Ralph Russell.

The cover depicts the sculpture *All Dressed Up and Nowhere To Go* by
Souheil Sleiman. Reproduced here by permission of the sculptor.

CONTENTS

for
Lily Vera

prologue: foreign bodies

The installation by Souheil Sleiman comprised a shallow heap of sand covering the floor of the Gallery with plastic bags placed over it. It was shown at Mafuji Gallery, Hackney, 2000; Zico House Beirut and Maarouf Saad Cultural Centre Sidon, 2001.

Private View

which is on the top floor of an industrial building. Here the 'art' goes to an edge, an edge that is brushed by our footsteps as we look down. I imagine being right down there and the sand's edge is like a cliff. Looking across at the bags, neatly arranged, maybe they would look like fields and farms. The thing is, do the bags hold the sand down or are they held down by it? Are they emerging from the sand or are they being buried beneath it?

What it made me think of was *Death in Venice*, the Visconti film. I thought of the Venice Lido, somewhere I have never been, towels and deckchairs neatly laid out suggested here by the striped and lettered plastic, a beach nostalgia with heavy Mahlerian music effects sinking down through the floor to the next stratum, that is the garment workers on the floor below. So here is the beach; in this country you have to pay to go there, you are arranged in rows and death comes down through the ceiling in a shower of plastic, like the ash descending on Pompeii, and this is what's left afterwards, this array of emptied out signs.

Later I thought of the time I read Chateaubriand's *Atala*, when I was at boarding school. Chateaubriand was an early French Romantic, an aristocrat and diplomat. All I can remember of the story is that it featured a romance between a traveller and Atala, a young Native American woman. Atala dies and the one detail from the book I can now recall is her burial. Her naked body is covered in earth but with one breast left protruding above the soil, pale against the dark earth, suggested by one of these plastic bags, as if this one image were what the world-weary traveller in pursuit of the exotic brought back, all the horrors of an emptied-out sign.

Older now still trying to read what the world says, commodification of an existence. And the gallery space? It was like a pacified ocean. The corporate art consultant was there. She had 'moved eastwards' she told me, and bought into a new canal-side development. As for the area, she gave it 'the next twenty years.'

So welcome to these excavations.

Street, Cemetery and Park

Marginal existence, flyblown hot light where the street is an edge. As if dressing up like that, tattoos and multiple piercings, might for a moment make you feel complete before the next stratum descends.

A field that fills with names. You can tell who are the 'well-loved' just by reading their inscriptions. Shall I inhabit this place with my name? In the smashed chapel there are fragments of light where the remaining fragments of glass hang from their lead tendrils—and the plants that sprout from the building's roof, it's as if they are waving to me. Here are millions of leaves, I shall sleep with the sound of them always in my ears. And sculpture's unending moment—but I have a question to ask. If a man stand still as a statue will be become?

In the park 'Do Not Disturb' the artist in her tent. All these recuperations of an existence. Two turtles, slow in their existence. I write this in leaf-light, leaning on the bridge. Animal cries of humans in distress as if they have been deserted by something. The signs on parade, but here is another one drifting towards me over the pavement bellied with wind. Let us consider the meanings, one by one, taking them home.

Abandoned Sites

The poem a site of lost meanings. Archaeology of a once-self, it hovers, a work that disappears and then re-appears where another exhibition opens at twilight and a subsidised music begins, here in another abandoned workshop. Making meaning, something swept up like that enormous weight of sand in the gallery.

You walked upstairs in a weekend silence moving towards an idea that had become an object, however briefly; past the polythene-wrapped garments on the floor below hanging there in rows like ghosts at attention. Up here at the top the walls are white and it leads you to think that you might travel to somewhere where the being of perfect silence is. As if the object might escape these signs and have no value. And the beach a halfway station where it stretches away, the lost signs emerging like Atala's breast.

british estate

Low rise, an off-white colour,
The walls a sort of scumbled finish.
It's opposite a cemetery,
Victorian. Overgrown.
'In 1966', the leaflet reads
'Relevant parts were freed
From the effects of consecration'.
A window lifts like a lid
Releasing the effects of music,
Its ethnicity not immediately apparent.

A globe set spinning in an empty classroom
Half the surface bruised with red—
As if the mistake still dogs our steps.
One summer afternoon I walked in there
Alone, among the scarcely legible dead
Arrived at a small clearing
A block of whitish stone, some strands of ivy
That clung there, instead of a name that might
Tell me what was buried in the ground
Beyond the reach of all that music.

Refugee

They'll come, from there to here.
No it is not a pilgrimage, this
Distance from you to I.
Relentless caravan,
The always being forced
To choose a different sky—
'I' wants to know where 'you' is from,
It wants your story
But you were so carefully folded
Into your own silences.

Once over here you're doing the dance of shadows
Hanging about the courts
Waiting for judgement,
Something to be 'handed down',
Ambiguous inheritance.

Festival

What they bring's a fluttering remnant,
Folk dance glimpsed through a doorway,
Men playing an endless game of cards.

We know them by their food,
Offerings as if to tempt us.
But that festival in the park—
It was a nation-in-waiting,
It was waiting under the trees
In steady English rain

And we were starting to wonder
Had they always been here
Condensing out of such emptiness
To speak in a different language,
Blamed mainly because they came near?

Here was a new kind of silence
Had somehow come to surround us
And *I am because of you* it was saying
The gap in the text the catch in the voice

And an alien music.

Screen

It has a semi-human face
Distilled on screens,
This thing that speaks in our name,

An approximation of something
Let loose on the world
And this is what it keeps on saying:

'You will pay for what I did to you
Again and again and again.'

The Singer

This was the singer
They have taken out his voice—
It must have been a mistake?
The voice that speaks itself
In a whisper now, just an inch above the ground

When a piece of earth comes flying.
Somewhere it had a name
Lost in the folds of a map.
Ownership thickened around it

And lives half guessed-at
Who'd imagined this piece of earth.
They peopled it with trees,
A sound here and there, as of running water,
Scents, seasons.
It is somewhere inside the map,
A map furled like a flag

And he is the news from nowhere
Who met with an accident of time—
Hold the microphone close to his face,
Enlarge the possibilities of speech,
He'll offer you his throat:

'I am the singer with the ruined face
The one grown hard to recognise.
How can you sit and watch like that?'
I'll stay here at the edge and wonder
How it might be for once to be all voice
And wait here on the page,
Such privileged existence!

Under Ground

Earls Court, the evening heat
Stretched out between the terraces
Where tourists pitch their tents.
Walking as if to nowhere in particular
This crowd has learned to look and eat and travel
All in the one movement.
But later in the Underground
Who could measure
The weight of his slack arms
Tattooed with 'England', a rose
And on each hand a spider's web?
You surface again
Somewhere just north of Piccadilly.
Its quite dark now, the vegetation
Is all behind plate glass.
Well-mannered jungle greens
Are shiny as briefcases.

Coalition

'A coalition of interests': information
Is dust in the eyes, a sandstorm approaching—
Those feathery trees start to wave.
At evening the soldiers are fed.

A journalist hears an explosion.
He peers shyly over the edge—
A word or two snatched from chaos
To settle here among ruins.

Does dust have a name, where it
Plucks out a cry?
Such being dust's currency, final flutter
In the eyes of a wounded intelligent animal,

Its intimations of a final stillness.
There was dereliction beyond the call of duty
And an architecture of chaos
The summer's height, its grinning numbers

Where a cloud, rising lazily
Like a curtain, is lifted away
An intelligence quick as a lizard
Still hanging on, somewhere among these ruins.

Ode

And mocked at by his own equipment
That's hard and good while he's decayed
Keith Douglas

Traces of a former encampment.
Something was burnt here, leaving
This residue where once there had been
The romance of all that perpetual moving about.
They were picturesque in their tents

And an English Arabist, with a tendency to betrayal
Was hovering somewhere there in the background—
'Towards evening we came to their booths'.
He was heading for 'the empty quarter'
And a country—it does make a nice shape on a map.

Because we have been translated
Being ferried across, well no
Not the waters of Lethe exactly,
But here, to where there are men on screens
Being confronted by their absent selves.

Before the war, just a moment before starting
The statues all stopped listening.
A ziggurat grew prosperous with shadows.
'Is it the war against everyone
And tell me please, has it started yet?'

Such emptily insistent voices,
The distance we carry inside us,
News from the embassy of nowhere

The words, that gather
Like a distant invisible army, now welcome him.

He'll bring you a sky growing dark with pamphlets
And streets turning grey as they dissolve to dust,
History like a time-lapse photograph.
We had swallowed almost all the news—
It's an old song sung in a freshly dug grave

But there is a kind of rhetoric digs its own grave.
There may be something outlasts itself,
Something extinct already, and it does not know it.
Perhaps it is an excavation
We're trying, each, to find our way out of.

The light, it is so much stronger than us
And the sky, growing bright in answer
To my perpetual enquiry, I had found these words
Like a garment to grow invisible in
Remaining suspended there.

how the city became its surface
A note on Raymond Mason

Bronze and fibreglass reliefs in a West End gallery. It's the paradox of the flat not-flat surface. These reliefs are intensely perspectival, rendered as perspective would be on a flat surface. At the same time of course they are three-dimensional but in a compressed way and the effect of this compression is of something suspended, intriguingly, between two and three dimensions. Distance is a sort of cheat and, notwithstanding this flatness, a surface can create its own shadows.

The bronze a dull grey-green, antique—but here in 'Barcelona Tram' it's the figure of a woman getting on to the tram and the way she seems to be flying into it, her skirt blowing out behind her. People caught in their poses, trapped in the vehicle's windows, betray such a sense of isolation. The tram resembles a classical façade, the shadows as of late afternoon, deep-set eyes, movement frozen into stillness. The people moving up and down the steps in the 'Place de l'Opéra'—the lines delineating their clothes are deeply incised and it's all set inside a sort of shallow box with one side, the lid you might say, having been lifted off. The steps look oddly precipitous and it's as if the figures are coming out towards you, floating away from the surface and you wonder, how can they possibly get up that flight of steps? There are all these heads afloat on bodies and for a moment they seem to be dancing.

'Man In Street' is just one man inexplicably singled out to stand for the 'crowd' and it's only his head. In here the traffic has been silenced, likewise the passers-by whose looks are waiting for you outside. In here we are brought closer to the altitude of our lives. Something makes our presence 'felt'. By the door on the way out are the big resin reliefs that represent entire cities, Paris, New York, London, cities moving towards the sky as I do as well, leaving the gallery, and here I am now on the page.

on 'murder mile'

        from where
In a voice of great purity it
            sometimes descends:

The cashpoint queue
          a shield of
Water reflecting the clouds
It's as if you were stepping over
The shallow face of a god

Their business it is to be out
There's the girl with the copper hair

A barrenness of waiting buds
Silence—it's just before the explosion

A life carefully balanced
Like the hat on his head

…

So it came to this poor ground

Maybe there are quite different bits of you
Climbing from one to the other
And something else lights up—
It climbs itself and
Here it is
Its arms spread wide

Walking the
Self   a history

And 'here'—it is simply
The way   its breath   divides the air

A cool arch
                    instep
The words collect in
As if as if as if

I will walk slowly back in there
Anxious not to disturb the dust—
The differing bits of 'you'
Are all the silences inside

…

That feeling   of an overpowering strangeness
It was like a perverse gift
                              Is it a child
Wondering if he's special?

Troubled   ecstasy of the self
Ecstasis   is standing outside?

But who was the stranger at the door
London in a blaze behind me
Blitz recalled in a dream
Dreamt more than fifty years ago?

There is nothing fixed in your eye
A shadow that prints itself

Leans forward into it   the amazing flesh

Struck Cup

                    The band struck up   it was
An unravelling sky
scraper
                    re
built?

It's a taking apart

And more fragile than we'd expected
Whose prismatic array
Transfixed the pedestrian
Still persistently moving about.

Fleeting mental states—as if
The desert, had entered the city
And it was as if to suggest
An opulence of emptiness:
                            Lebanon in my heart—
I saw the words, carved into a cactus
By a roadside once in Athens

In Hackney Wick the sculptor spoke
Who had gathered these fragments of mirror
Stitched them together, as if they were
Gravestones set in the sky

Back home, in a silence made of walls
I shuffled around my house
Persistence   breezy summer
Bosomy bright-edged clouds
But the plunge, and the re-emergence
Shards in its hair
                    imagine:

This shattered medusa
The word tricks it finds
A kind of ground   and me?
I come after and here's where I am
Like a handkerchief, pulled out
By an empty-faced magician
Out from a ring out of nowhere

The way each child's so perfectly contained
In that small pool of self

Else in full leaf the trees
                          this stooping rush

Each piece of mirror, that's
Cracked at the margin

...

Alexandria: is it
Towards a city
But defunct—that can
Swim or sprout eyes

Library   lighthouse   drowned statues
On the balcony   stands there   a stranger
The name is   lips kissing themselves

Where the sculpture arrives
In its packing case

Flatpack assembly:
Dismembered to two dimensions

And under the sea   someone's here
Making a shape out of something lonely

It has eyes instead of a name
In the harbour of drowning

Inimical still to the texture of flesh
It's a carapace sloughed off

A thing of endless corners
Look backward   the usual stranger

So perched it in my mind
Where everything leaves its faint print

But somewhere's the shape of a human
'Come over here and be loved'

And a voice, that might last in the calling
From 'somewhere out of Africa'

Smashed to a dazzle—my animal mouth
Being walked here into a mirror's silence

...

There is a sort of wound   imagine
Is what's not visible between us
'Empire' was the wound
It was dealt from such a distance

It crosses an uncertain border
Between sense and estrangement.
There is a threshold you touch and are touched by
To practise being grateful—
We are often polite, fall silent about it
But here in my small mind
It is, it weighs me down
Like a distant explosion—
Looking all around, it left
Not one unwounded here

Tattered flight 'light bone structure
Number of wing-beats per second'
Later the trees closed round shrapnel
In its aftermath of silence
You were watching them put out more leaves

Waking up, the dream—
It was like something dark in a puddle of light
How in the early light
All things seeming possible
A taking possession of someone else's silence

Yes but everywhere you go
This city—it looks back at you
Through fractured lenses

He returned, with a splash, this man with his salutation
It's a sort of greeting   an animal sound
The stateliness and violence

Out of the sun, towards me, along the street
This shadow   something hooded
And all of its history
Half-buried somewhere behind it
And this one, he comes up behind you
An offcut of that silence:
'Empty out your pockets!'

In the anxiety of afternoon

                              taking it up again
To share my space

                              a felt answer—
You who are always near me
Making 'door music'

Visiting Exile

'They are like us'
But are we like us?

'You are because I am'
Is it I owe him my life?

Condition of exile's
An echo that starts in the ear
Brick builds itself on brick
Wall climbs   a swaying performance
Bodies slip out   through cracks in its understanding

I'd discarded the days like an alien narrative

Language: an echo that starts in the flesh

And so began its prose:

YOU

Feeling so ill-at-ease in the place where you were, you found
this other place where you could go. They make you welcome
there—maybe it's because they are grateful that you have taken
the trouble to come to them. You imagine how their pain
might become yours. One day perhaps one of them will say,
'Now you are one of us' and you will feel profoundly gratified.
This contact you have makes you feel special when you come
back to your own place. But of course there is this important
difference between you and them—you do have somewhere
to go back to at any time. Meanwhile you sit outside and
watch the language they have. You might imagine being found
here, in this other language, and feeling 'Now at last I can be

myself'—so whose self were you before? Even that part of you that you feel can never quite be reached, you imagine that one day it might be completely and utterly spoken.

HIM

The silent ache of afternoon and I seem to see him lift himself from sleep, splash water on his face. There's the way the light seems to choose each particular reflection, how it's caught on the tap's metal with such bright authority where he looks out over our rooftops, waking to them each day as if it were to an illness. He was floated across impossible borders to settle here like an unmarked milestone, his arrival here the final weight of a door.

It was I who had helped him make this translation. Stranded halfway over a bridge each looked for himself in a different language. There was something that hovered between us. Signs, as if they were carved out of air, and something I must not turn my back on. Is it a self imperfectly remembered? Substantial breathing form, it dwindles into a mirror and I am being turned away from the blankness and its all-seeing stare, am joined once again to the beleaguered crowd.

He was old when I found him
Alone among the things of the world

He and I bundled together—
I'm practising my stances

And the start of my forgetting, it is
Right here inside my head

lyrical cities

We were not far short
of remote Sarabad
and stopped to confer

And the bells,
the arches, seen
from cobalt balconies
even before we found the gate
(is it desert in there?)
Are there no walls?
(once touched they recede)
Where is the tower?
(blanched in the shining.)
And where,
where are your people—
                    Abdulkarim Kasid,
                    translated by the poet with David Kuhrt

The poet Ghalib was in Delhi in 1857 when the city was taken
over by the rebels and the Mughal Emperor was proclaimed
ruler once again. One of Ghalib's functions had been to act
as *ustad* or poetic mentor to the old emperor, a scholarly man
and a poet, who by this time had lost all his real power to the
British. When the British re-took the city Ghalib was brought
before one Colonel Burn. The Colonel asked him in bad Urdu,
"You Moslem?" "Half", replied the poet. "I don't eat pork, but
I drink wine." It was claret that he drank, mixed with two parts
rosewater. In the hot weather he would sit on the roof of his
house until late in the night while he worked out his verses.
Each time he completed a verse he would tie a knot in a sash.
The next day when he picked up the sash, each knot reminded
him of a verse and he would write it down. In Dastanbuy, his
account of the uprising in Delhi, he wrote: "In this upheaval I
have had no part in any matter of policy. I simply carried on
with my verse-correcting." But, describing the sack of the city
by British soldiers, he wrote of a nearby house belonging to a
nobleman of his acquaintance: 'From the roof at midnight, I

could see everything in the light of the leaping flames, and feel
... the ash falling on my body ... Songs sung in a neighbour's
house are, as it were, gifts which it sends; how then should fire
in a neighbour's house not send gifts of ashes?'

Ghalib on his rooftop
          knots in his sash
The stars' accustomed brilliance, impeccable verses

'You can see the whole city from here'
A city that was presumed to exist
Where it hovered, an inch above the plain

City streets today
Are a spaciousness of trees

It was 'I' in its emptying streets
Nostalgia for presence   frail passenger

And every furtive creature
Bird trapped in our vine, a wall dense with grapes

A smell of ash
                came drifting across

And that was all
Standing in front of silence like a prayer

...

At school in East London a boy who had come from Lahore wrote this: *One day I was watching my best pigeon flying over the sky, here and there in the evening. My father came to me and called my name, but I was only aware of the evening, therefore I didn't hear anything. Then he shouted 'Jimi'—that was my nickname—'Listen, I am going to take you to London tomorrow.'*

In the armour of flight   they are
Scything the air of its moments
Rebirth, in a different tongue
Pigeon going here and there in the sky
Each evening he called the bird home
Now it flies off and into a separate darkness
His pocket is empty, touches him everywhere

Bird-man toppling inwards
Fell into a city of looks
Otherhood, sanctuary, soft as a name
Uttered at nightfall—
                              the wound
            closed
To descend
            such a rush of air—
A body fell out of the sky.
On the way down it sprouted wings
And here it is now, stocky fortunate angel
Abandoned its sky-refuge

The garden swept clean
The gardener paused on his broom
Flowers rescued from a skip
A self as if cradled beyond harm

Or
      spilt
It seems to come
From somewhere further off
                    fantastic hungers!

A bird trapped in a vine
Quickness of head and eye

Who am not a reliable witness
With that peculiar darting mind
Its play of revelations

And here's the poor
Art its
         crown—

Up early   trying the silence
As if I could hold it all in my hand
It moves away   once touched
Into much too comfortable verse

I never looked for it and still it found me
'The words will all take care of themselves'
A song imprisoned in a room
And a voice that's partly mine?

We're launched in a foreign wind
Who exist these many deaths
A city fallen into ruin's
                    bewitching paths

Here where they did not know what they'd become
They shout their programme
And bodies, fallen out of use—
It's what the world is made of. Famous bird!

Look up—a faint screaming,
Yes those are swifts
Making their sky meal
And the inward fortifications?

Well, I had made myself lonely

the wedding party

Escaping judgement, here
On foreign soil—
Outside the Embassy's a dead patrol.
Sweeping the pavement his
Yellow tabard reads 'Enterprise'

Once seated inside
"maximum occupancy load"
"no input detected"
Dead words the reconstructed air
As we *dialogue with each other*

folks not integrated into the world economy

And a language blanket
Clausewitz   the fog of war
there's the 'stuff happens' stuff

not more difficult he said
but a shorter road to success

but like us having the same global reach

...

Hamlet:
  'my people—
To keep them from sleep'
Captain Hawkins a fish dinner
Off the coast of Africa
A question is   which quarto?

Emperor Fish House   Eden Music   Salon de Thé
In West Green Road Tottenham
Kumasi Central Market   Perfect News
Uncle Snooker Social Club

The shape of a language
The poop deck   a theatre
Carried it all that way
And Empire a sort of confidence trick
A thing of shadows, half-selves

The language gathered them
Into its ambiguous embrace
They sweated out its syllables

Come, freshen me   start with my mouth
The inrush and going towards it
Half an assault and half an embrace

& a face half burnt—it
Was shaped to a beak like a bird's

Something was heard, in the distance
A vague marching music

Here comes the wedding party
Winding its way to the desert

As if joining the proper queue for language
A tradition arriving, it drags its robes,

But something there is, whose roar fills the sky
Is a word breathed to the desert

And it opens, drinking its fill

'no joining fee'

Cropped skull and tattooed flesh
Irreducible   deserves elegy

In what it lived it lacked glory. But here
Impurities of blood's a sacred mixture,

A city where they'd brought their lives to be changed
'The horizon it was that changed me'

Sun on the bridge's shoulder
There must be a way home from here?

So are you 'they' and
Is it the bleeding stump of silence?
It's something on your wrist that's fed with husks.

The language is a lost cause, it hangs in the air
Like snow on the tongue
Like a hawk fed to the sky
And we are not quite music yet,

But
   'nothing can add beauty to light'
Its silent armour
And the tree in its springtime cage of blossom
A cage whose bars sing the answer—
The words as if pleased to arrive
They looked back up at me I
Clawed the text

A rising tide of reflections
Is dabbled in by light
Dismembered arch a murdered shadow

But radiance of the ordinary
Is something like a veil.
It is as commonplace as rain

At four o'clock there are
Hints of an abandoned richness
A cracked glass to remember it by

Here, smell my writing hand

...

Is it someone wearing a badge,
Is sad behind a logo, a sort of failed dignity?
It's on his back where he can't reach to scratch,
A man who slows, where summer wastes
An enormous strength down here.
The building workers, ranged along a wall
Are bodies being as if
Each sculpted out of idleness
And into a frieze of moments
Tattooed, like something
That waits to be deciphered
And a single ear ring's cheeky gold.
The dust each man
Is carrying in his skin
In every fold and crevice
Will be washed off as if it were the money
That flows away from him.

But now for a moment something
Archaic comes to mind
Here in the noon silence,
Its sense of a commanding presence.

home ground

Our cities shared their poisons with us
Saadi Youssef. Translated by Khaled Mattawa.

Cabbage white on the buddleia
Its humble energies of flight

Upside down city
A bird posed in the air

The difficult it is
Here, the original place?

Where nothing is fixed in the eye
A crust of buildings

Brick idyll   is only
What fails to disappear

Towerblock   Palmyra   a column
Hesitates   the blue

And here and there each
Self-important head

Drought in the mouth's a
Discussion of insects

And a sense of afternoon
This sober ecstasy of clouds

Poetry in small doses
In oracle language

Emptily dazzled   eyes
The readers stand in front, each takes it in turn.

How to travel here without heads?
How to sing
                without heads
Into an emptying circle?

It's a piece of a curtain
A bit of a tongue

NO HAND SIGNALS

Fell back   its
Uneven trajectory

Contented it
self with its echo

So the harmless
Days passed
And the bird   swung
    down
                                    momently
Am its arrival
Whose claws, here
                darken the page

Here he is, today, feeling empty and kind
Calling it here like a separate sound

Pressing the button marked Plenty
He's out there, gone looking, his favourite word

'The poet's arrival in the city'
He's puffed with foolish song

'Tarnished famine brilliance'
Self-quoting   went out to look for more words:

'blood clart police virgin' he's on the bus
Someone shouting into an empty phone

Live in a world of your own
A world that you own?

'They're only doing their shopping'
Each faithful dismembered carcass

Sheep's head looks down from a shelf
Propped cowfoot, thinks

'There is more wealth than I can manage'

...

Londonistan this
Othered I's
Home earth
To die in the land
Being 'laid to rest'
But torn away here
How shallow are
The roots of understanding

As if powdered with their names
Gutturals I strove to utter
Here in an East London classroom
Ripening like a bed of fruit
I don't defend the process
Ashes that float across
This soft-voiced alien narrative
Dying in history's echo

Here they are in the post office—
As if they were queuing at the end of empire

It is a
              convenient flag
'Language'

Well we'll all
                   arrive someday

Silent alternative
                   layers of ash
And outside a new kind of
                   facade is proposed
As if signing the
                   dust with our names

The poem in a voice that's not quite mine
And as to what gave rise   its
                   random flight
'the poet's arrival in the city'
Steps becoming substance,

                                        words this
Wretched afflatus!

Who did his best with the
Intractable substance
It glistens inside—
Ambiguous shape-shifting country
As every honest citizen avers
In some desert and
                        here is its language

the balcony

Londonistan
               america fundamental
'get me out of here'

Arms up comes out
                    onto a balcony
Naked almost
               what it aspires to
Self-abolition
          a dissolved sign

'Come out of there, and we . . .
We will not shoot you this time'

A man wrapped in paper a paper man
Wearing remains of an immortal book
'Yes. We can read you like a book!'

Hands over its flesh,
Was once a warm embrace

And did not want to touch
Something so shrivelled, it
                   speaks?

'English, like a curse'
And it was as if I'd invented a person
Alterior voice
And I had begun him
Is it   naked on a balcony
Is it a word or a man?
Whose wounded appetites, remote as music—

A compound man already
Haunting the future—

Being all potential is
A gathering-point of forces

And half-way to being, in another tongue
Where exile prints its name

Shallow
            magnificence
In the twinkling of an eye
It is like an illness you'll discover
Just go out there and scream!

The night speaker
Uneasy exuberance of its streets
Were what I had to cross, to a room full of presence
The curtain swayed evening sunlight pouring in
Pulse of the city   beyond

Out here is your ground
As if waiting
For there to be less
                        wretched afflatus!
And yes, the

Relief of less
Look in there you can see him
He begins to write as if something depended on it
And if I could come to rest
In you this final hour

After the rain
An awkward gleam
A minor alteration in the air
And a sort of redundant vigour
Here he is the thief of voices

Dismembered with a prayer
Harks back, to the original sacrifice
Furtive imprecations
Gutters swimming with sewage
Stories   I mean

The man's impossible dignity
Cornered in exile
Is what fails to disappear
Dumb partner to the animal
And said to the reader, vanish

Turning the page
                              pulled down the lid
                              climbing inside

...

The water in the canal is fairly clear
Swan family their
Bliss of extended necks

And the way a column ends abrupt as that
A failing arrow gathers speed
And the future's almost here

As if straining for effect the fruit hangs down
Blunted municipal mosaics
Tagging   miraculous inscriptions

The water comes alive with light
On the underside of the bridge
Is where the water prints itself as light

Aspiring   respiring   trees imagining fruit
It almost touches the water
Such ripeness descending

It sinks beyond reach
Buried in its reflection
In passing shop windows

...

Empty clatter of leaves blown over the square
Waiting to cross the road one's hunched and veiled
And who was suddenly there
Beside me and we were no longer young
As if self were a city and we are all other—
Just to be like that in the air
Abrupt as a bird's life and it is enough.
Each one of them holds the secret of its flight
And as if no longer knowing myself
I stumbled, she lifted her face and I saw
One who spoke in a flutter of lips, as if limping in english
Her hand was like a claw!
'And I see it, your news takes possession'
Veiled, hardly visible, importuning me, sister of ash
Spreading her arms and the absence between us,

Some cloth, a tinge of blood,
Faint elderly warmth, to fade, with its
Dignity into its ground

untold wealth

At night we found a deserted city
Water ran under the streets
The houses dry and full of herbs
                    Roland Penrose

The new city borderless
Its city gates become a set of shadows.

It's an empire built out of signs
And a place of odd meaningless arenas.

'Palladiums are where it rightly lives'
Empty lyric performance.

Electrum gleam in river sand
Was a king with a mouth of gold—

A ritual to open the statue's mouth
Put back the tongue and a sturdy measure

To circle the metal's rough substance?
Dead legend. Missing it now

Although I was bathed in its light
And a stadium whispered its crowds

I who went out walking
As if I were scarcely begun

Imagined scattering coins
In this city of future ruins.

Here is one spun in the air   brief shine
Its lyric gleam

Enough of it's   to fall   here's scarcely a sound
There's a god surely who sits in the air

But being here entirely without substance
The trick of it's keeping the thing in the air.

Like the scribble of smoke from a sacrifice
It finds a way to the sky.

Screen-flicker translates into riches
Hidden carefully somewhere else behind trees.

Here, flights of capital   pigeons
They're turning turning on a depthless sky.

a poem of this poem

Fresco, being when the moment dries—
A god's apology?
A creature exits into leaf
And here's another, Apollo
Bowing before the sacrificial flesh
Stripping away the close-packed text,
Language turned inside out. And now
What kind of garment is it
Hung over branches, stiffening as it dries?

He lifts himself away from this
And turns to face the city
That opens in the distance like a sort of dream:

'Hoof clippings?' someone wrote,
'Ours is a cautious silence of rooms.
And days spent trying not to be angry.'

In here we can no longer smell the music
But still these deathless-seeming early mornings,
Birds in small unexpected flocks
Planes dozing in the sky
The language being transformed
Where tongue sits in its mouth,
The voice of flesh. Is it
That in the end we might be saved from harm?

Vague wandering suburb, trying to find
Just where it was it started.
March. Deadheads of last year's buddleia.
Each spring some stuff springs out.
There are feral daffodils.
They nod in the strict sunshine,

And trains that pull in to almost deserted platforms.
This is the land for the town
Its casual annihilation of a landscape,
A scatter of coins that spill from a broken pot.

'Even clean hands damage surfaces.'

The return to origins—before purities were befouled by words.
Before the ingrate word makers turned the artist's own symbols
against him with a 'what does it mean?
The sculptor David Smith, at Tate Modern 2006–07

Thin flat forest   lumpy bird
Art shared out among the millions
They arrive   with their awkward bodies,

Bodies that strive to be different
Clay's mystic mess, the garden of forms—
'This work and I whole nights together'

And now a sculpture, where it stands,
Among its seeming-still of shadows.
There was water stretching in front, narrative glitter.

Something came, breaking the surface
And after so much silence
It arrived like a small mountain.

Starting in on it
We could see the game it was playing.
'I'm making a name for myself up here'

But arriving at the event there was nobody there
Just those enormous empty photographs.
Imagine walking through it, texting the dead.

As the day gives out light shrinks to where we are
A plain prose surface, comfortable-seeming,
'As if it were a city I'd befriended'

And a world as if it knew itself without us,
Its careful scatterings of leaves.
Still, we survived the event

Here in the city we made, sculpture our fetishised sadness.

at home

Low trees bus drivers beware
Poor cornered animal

The face shines clear
Always read the label   grief

The way the other might
Return you to yourself

Anyway why do you need all those tunes?
A bird's quizzical stare

And your life, a sort of
Half-hearted quest

And finds a
Kind of ground, to practise here being grateful

Waking from time to time, to a
Happiness you hardly dare to touch?

Out walking early was the best of it
Walking through London

As if the city
Breathed itself towards you

As if language a membrane were flexible
& the night leaning in

Like an intake of breath
Past the leaves that shelter my window—

Leaves of a strong-growing vine
Sirens are safely outside

Too many words
Abrade the silence

Upbraid the silence? A fox is calling
And I only wanted to listen

To what the others see
As if we were travelling

All with one common purpose
Your gentle storm of breath in my ear

Maybe I'm in the words like a thumbprint
At home in my strangeness

and you

A form of address, to distance
Who wants to possess this thing calling it other.
It hovers in his mouth,
Possession biding its time
Here in a half-forgotten city
And last seen walking through it
A refugee from silence
Still talking to himself.
From time to time he'd write things down
In the small notebook that he always carries.
The sun's a brief token of light
On a tower block window
Over on the park's far side
Bringing the distance near
And now he gazes out as if
Across the sea, its
Easy consolation of distance—
'You have that faraway look in your eyes'
Hoping that so much concentration
Might open lips and all this time
The sense of self
Like something persisting in memory
And seeking the solution still—
As if left long enough
Waiting inside the mouth
It might dissolve into an answer.

yearn glass

'cut a long story'
                Souheil Sleiman

cracked glaze song

I constructed a journey

soothed the inner chaos

slanting afternoon sun

eased the ice   and it started again

a mouthful of cheap wine

defunct maleness

made out of dust and sunlight

we thought it might be art

reborn   in other air

imaginary return such being

the distances we live

mother without lips

one or two of whose names

the walls of whose prison escape me

leaves only a column of air

'erotic reminiscence'

went inwards   the debt to inside

finds and loses the centre

it smells of itself

the blankness beneath a mirror's

compelling glaze its settled glare

still wrapped / rapt in the gaze

a nimbus of gratification

a piece of my life

I won't take the rest

but stand back and wait

body of paint and a self-trace

thinks itself into the mirror

is nearer the animal

the flesh is outside

imagine it touches the glass

flesh makes a smear

abolishing distance

it leaves us here drowning in air

blond wood   now thirsting in tremendous light

mirror's ironic tilt

it's my limping survival

to outwit substance

big in name only

it'll settle the matter of depth

here in the mirror's margin

as these are my behaviour

valueless depth

its paradox depthlessness

now lumbers towards you

sing the frame I am sailing

into the ground

and an unsteady peace

when it stopped its signal

it is a kind of cold flame

left one of us here drowning

one of us saved from drowning

(the being-reflected's at the back of it)

as if it were another fine day

of purposeless striding

hesitates to the blue

something taunting the skyline

a clouded fingernail

it's 'all dressed up and nowhere to go'

and, finally, found a friend

twin hinges of

occulted light

they were all to each other

mirror and its reflection:

                   s / he

infant   sweet shit-smelling rose

perfect harbinger

echo   pleated voice

the way she sinks into the ground

mirror's abrupt gaze—

waving part of yourself goodbye

my friend and I

a slow arrival

for a long time circling the spot

to make the sign of absence

the bit of self-mirror I carry inside

reflections that take refuge

such a carapace

so cut a long story

a drop of blood

swells on the glass

mirror—each bloodless encounter

and you cannot see the join

as if a mirror turned round in the air

and found its way back into you

fractured glare

whose reflection divides me

it's a place of defunct fountains

a surface mirrors the breeze

but is it being human

to move here in such a dress?

needing a mirror to hang his silence in
the mirror cracked with all that noise
a babel of reflections

these pieces, made into an answer
with nothing behind it
it's 'all dressed up and nowhere to go'

yes it's brisk in this light,
reflection's denial of substance
as the city unravels

here's a mirror that turns you away
the anti-narcissus machine
it drinks up the ground

disappears into distant dry hills
an insubstantial tower's
glass wall will remember

and afterwards here in Mirror City
mirror will drink you and drink you
return you the stranger you are to yourself

its short glitter
                    dismantled
it's piled up on the gallery floor

self-quoting   the mirror
'tells each of me who I am'
a footnote. I hurried away

as if having
escaped from the earth
I had learned how to float

while seen from the bridge
late at night here is a man
in shirtsleeves, still working

immigrant   guardian   watcher
in his uniform   steps out
to look at all those lights

how all this silence tires
consigned to the light quarries
daytime's a hurry of selves going past

a garb of glass
in its vest of lights
a machine of money

and I could be
cast down like him into silence
what's here on the gallery floor

whose glass is
fused sand is
the dust at the heart of an explosion

Notes

'All Dressed Up And Nowhere To Go', the cover image for the book, is a sculpture by the London-based Lebanese artist Souheil Sleiman, and is a presence at various points in the text, most obviously in the sections 'Struck Cup' and 'Yearn Glass'. This work comprises hundreds of fragments of mirror attached to a framework of chicken wire. The artist has described how he started as a student working with textiles and he has become interested in the idea of *unravelling*. The work is a glass tower, like a glass skyscraper that is unravelling as if something has been taken apart and simplified, or a wall of mirrors which, as a financial centre, offers a distorted reflection, something apparently massive and solid which turns out to be vulnerable in more ways than one. And there is also the traditional idea that someone reflected in a mirror is still there, in the mirror, after s/he has gone . . .

British Estate
This is the name of a housing estate next door to Tower Hamlets cemetery in East London. The cemetery is now a nature reserve.

How the city became its surface
Raymond Mason is a Birmingham-born sculptor long resident in Paris; this section refers to an exhibition of his work at Marlborough Galleries.

Murder Mile
A stretch of Lower Clapton Road in Hackney became known at one point as 'murder mile' because of a series of shootings there.

Struck Cup
'The sculptor spoke . . .' and references to Alexandria: Souheil Sleiman's 'All Dressed Up . . .' (see note above) was one of Lebanon's official entries for the Alexandria Biennale in November 2007,

Lyrical Cities
Abdulkarim Kasid is an Iraqi poet living in London.

Ghalib was a major Urdu poet in the 19th Century. In 'Dastanbuy' ('A Posy of Flowers'), his account of his time in Delhi before and after the sacking of the city by the British in 1857 he wrote:

Now every English soldier that bears arms
Is sovereign and free to work his will.

Men dare not venture out into the street
And terror chills their hearts within them still.

Their homes enclose them as in prison walls
And in the Chauk the victors hang and kill.

The city is athirst for Moslem blood
And every grain of dust must drink its fill.

Translated by Ralph Russell

Some twenty years later, reflecting on these same events, Sir Alfred Lyall, Governor of the Punjab, wrote in *Studies at Delhi 1876*:

Hardly a shot from the gate we stormed,
　　Under the Moree battlement's shade;
Close to the glacis our game was formed,
　　There had the fight been, and there we played.

　Lightly the demoiselles tittered and leapt,
　　Merrily capered the players all;
North, was the garden where Nicolson slept,
　　South was the sweep of a battered wall.

Near me a Musalman, civil and mild,
  Watched as the shuttlecocks rose and fell;
And he said, as he counted his beads and smiled,
  'God smite their souls to the depths of hell.'

The Wedding Party
Hamlet: my people . . . In 1607 ship's captain William Keeling, becalmed off the coast of Sierra Leone, described in the ship's Logbook how he 'invited Captain Hawkins' from another ship 'to a fish dinner, and had Hamlet acted aboard me; which I permit to keep my people from idleness and unlawful games, or sleep.'

Home Ground
'Londonistan' is a term is said to have been coined by a member of the French secret services because London was allegedly harbouring Islamists.

Saadi Youssef is an Iraqi poet living in London.

Untold Wealth
'Future ruins' refers to the drawing by the architect John Soane's assistant, Joseph Gandy, where Gandy imagines Soane's Bank of England as a ruin.

According to Herodotus, 'the Lydians were the first people we know to have struck and used coinage of silver and gold.' He states that these first coins were of Croesus, King of Lydia. Their coins were made of electrum, a natural alloy of silver and gold found in the riverbed.

'Palladiums are where it rightly lives' is a line is from a poem by Allen Fuchs. The palladium: 'The image of the goddess Pallas, in the citadel of Troy, on which the safety of the city was supposed to depend, reputed to have been brought thence to Rome' (OED)

A Poem of this Poem

This section makes reference to the Domenicino frescoes originally made for the Aldobrandini Villa, a number of which are now in the National Gallery, (where at the time of writing they could be seen only on Wednesday afternoons and not always then.) They depict the achievements of the god Apollo. The god is shown attacking a succession of primitive, more or less defenceless creatures—the Cyclops, the satyr Marsyas, Daphne and so on. In one fresco, 'Apollo and Neptune advising Laodemon on the Building of Troy', the god appears as a celestial town planner while the New City rises, immaculate, in the distance. These scenes are depicted as if on tapestry hangings. At the foot of one of them and standing just in front of it, obscuring the fringed edge, is a burly dwarf, chained and staring out at the spectator, holding his manacled wrists in front of him.

Yearn Glass

'Yearn Glass' was the name of a mirror manufacturer whose premises were next door to Souheil Sleiman's former studio in Hackney Wick. 'Cut a long story' was written across a fragment of broken mirror by the artist.

www.ingramcontent.com/pod-product-compliance
Lightning Source LLC
Chambersburg PA
CBHW031932080426
42734CB00007B/657